GOD SO LOVED THE WORLD

Reflections on the Beauty of God's Creation

editor
Maryjane Hooper Tonn

•

managing editor
Lorraine Obst

•

art editor
Ralph Luedtke

ACKNOWLEDGMENT: "Love all God's creation . . ." from THE BROTHERS KARAMAZOV
by Feodor Dostoyevsky, translated from the
Russian by Constance Garnett. Copyright
1912. Used by permission of William
Heinemann Ltd., Publishers, and also
Macmillan Publishing Co., Inc.

GOD SO LOVED
THE WORLD...

In the beginning God
created the heaven
and the earth.
Genesis 1:1

THE STORY OF CREATION

And God said, Let the waters under the heaven be gathered together unto one place, and let the dry land appear: and it was so.

And God called the dry land Earth; and the gathering together of the waters called he Seas: and God saw that it was good.

And God said, Let the earth bring forth grass, the herb yielding seed, and the fruit tree yielding fruit after his kind, whose seed is in itself, upon the earth: and it was so.

And the earth brought forth grass, and herb yielding seed after his kind, and the tree yielding fruit, whose seed was in itself, after his kind: and God saw that it was good.

And the evening and the morning were the third day.

And God said, Let there be lights in the firmament of the heaven to divide the day from the night; and let them be for signs, and for seasons, and for days, and years:

And let them be for lights in the firmament of the heaven to give light upon the earth: and it was so.

And God made two great lights; the greater light to rule the day, and the lesser light to rule the night: he made the stars also.

And God set them in the firmament of the heaven to give light upon the earth,

And to rule over the day and over the night, and to divide the light from the darkness: and God saw that it was good.

And the evening and the morning were the fourth day.

And God said, Let the waters bring forth abundantly the moving creature that hath life, and fowl that may fly above the earth in the open firmament of heaven.

And God created great whales, and every living creature that moveth, which the waters brought forth abundantly, after their kind, and every winged fowl after his kind: and God saw that it was good.

And God blessed them, saying, Be fruitful, and multiply, and fill the waters in the seas, and let fowl multiply in the earth.

And the evening and the morning were the fifth day.

And God said, Let the earth bring forth the living creature after his kind, cattle, and creeping thing, and beast of the earth after his kind: and it was so.

And God made the beast of the earth after his kind, and cattle after their kind, and every thing that creepeth upon the earth after his kind: and God saw that it was good.

And God said, Let us make man in our image, after our likeness: and let them have dominion over the fish of the sea, and over the fowl of the air, and over the cattle, and over all the earth, and over every creeping thing that creepeth upon the earth.

So God created man in his own image, in the image of God created he him; male and female created he them.

And God blessed them, and God said unto them, Be fruitful, and multiply, and replenish the earth, and subdue it: and have dominion over the fish of the sea, and over the fowl of the air, and over every living thing that moveth upon the earth.

Genesis 1:9-28

This is the day which
the Lord hath made; we will
rejoice and be glad in it.

Psalm 118:24

The world is God's epistle to mankind…his thoughts
are flashing upon us from every direction.

Plato

It is a wholesome and necessary thing
for us to turn again to the earth and
in the contemplation of her beauties
to know the sense of wonder and humility.

Rachel Carson

Earth, with her thousand voices, praises God.

Samuel Taylor Coleridge

My sisters the birds, much are ye beholden unto God, your Creator, and always and in every place, ought ye to praise Him, because He hath given you liberty to fly wheresoever ye will, and hath clothed you on with twofold and threefold raiment.

St. Francis of Assisi

Earth, thou great footstool of our God, who reigns
on high…thou fruitful source of all our raiment, life,
and food…our house, our parent, and our nurse.

Isaac Watts

The best way to know God is to love many things.
Vincent van Gogh

If you wisely invest in beauty, it will remain
with you all the days of your life.
Frank Lloyd Wright

All the rivers run into the sea
yet the sea is not full
unto the place from whence the rivers come
thither they return again.

Ecclesiastes 1:7

There is a serene and settled majesty in woodland scenery
that enters into the soul and delights and elevates it,
and fills it with noble inclinations.

Washington Irving

When I would beget content, and increase con-
fidence in the power and wisdom and providence
of Almighty God, I will walk in the meadows of
some gliding stream, and there contemplate the
lilies that take no care, and those very many
other little living creatures that are not only
created but fed (a man knows not how) by the
goodness of the God of nature, and therefore
trust in Him.

Izaak Walton

Never lose an opportunity of seeing
anything that is beautiful; for beauty
is God's handwriting...a wayside sacrament.
Ralph Waldo Emerson

No ray of sunlight is ever lost, but the green
which it awakens into existence needs time to sprout,
and it is not always granted to the sower to see
the harvest. All work that is worth anything
is done in faith.

Albert Schweitzer

Only the day dawns
to which we are awake.
Henry David Thoreau

Love all God's creation, the whole and every grain of sand in it. Love every leaf, every ray of God's light. Love the animals, love the plants, love everything. If you love everything, you will perceive the divine mystery in things. Once you perceive it, you will begin to comprehend it better every day, and you will come at last to love the whole world with an all-embracing love.

Feodor Dostoyevsky

Nature is the art of God.
Dante Alighieri

The perfection of any matter, the highest or the lowest, touches on the divine.

Martin Buber

God made the flowers to beautify the earth and cheer man's careful mood; and he is happiest who hath power to gather wisdom from a flower, and wake his heart in every hour to pleasant gratitude.

William Wordsworth

I love all beauteous things,
I seek and adore them;
God hath no better praise,
And man in his hasty days
Is honoured for them.
                    Robert Bridges

O Lord, how manifold are thy works!
in wisdom hast thou made them all:
the earth is full of thy riches.

Psalm 104:24

In all ranks of life
the human heart yearns for the beautiful
and the beautiful things that God makes
are His gift to all alike.

Harriet Beecher Stowe

The trees,
like the longings of the earth,
stand atiptoe
to peep at the heaven.
Rabindranath Tagore

For God so loved the world, that he gave his only begotten Son, that whosoever believeth in him should not perish, but have everlasting life.

St. John 3:16

The summer comes and the summer goes…
Wild flowers are fringing the dusty lanes,
The swallows go darting through fragrant rains,
Then, all of a sudden, it snows.

Thomas Bailey Aldrich

God grant me the serenity to accept the things
I cannot change…courage to change the things
I can…and wisdom to know the difference.

Reinhold Niebuhr

Let every dawn of morning be to you as the beginning of life, and every setting sun be to you as its close; then let every one of these short lives leave its sure record of some kindly thing done for others, some goodly strength or knowledge gained for yourself.

John Ruskin

<big>H</big>e hath made
every thing beautiful
in his time…
Ecclesiastes 3:11